Freelancer Writer's Anatomy

Becoming a Successful Freelancer from Idea to Pay Cheque

By Louise F. Blank

FREELANCE WRITER'S ANATOMY

Written by Louise F. Blank

Library and Archives Canada Cataloguing in Publication

Blank, Louise, 1954-, author

Freelancer writer's anatomy: from idea to pay cheque--how I

became a successful freelancer / by Louise F. Blank.

Electronic monograph in HTML format.

ISBN 978-0-9808958-1-0 (html)

1. Authorship--Vocational guidance. 2. Freelance journalism--

Vocational guidance. 3. Feature writing--Vocational guidance.

I. Title.

PN153.B53 2016   808'.02   C2016-903996-X

For every writer who dares to push their words out the door.

TABLE OF CONTENTS

Chapter 1 – First Anatomy Lesson

Freelance writers are like athletes in training. Brainstorming, writing, researching, and editing are workout routines for your writing brain. Brains work like a vehicle's GPS. Before they can give directions, they need to know your destination. The freelance writing routines for generating an article proposal in this book remind your brain of your destination. In return, it provides the best directions.

Many of my students and others struggling to achieve their writing dreams attribute the struggle to an anatomy deficit. There are no holes in your anatomy and mom didn't forget to put writing genes in your milk. What you may need is an understanding of how to guide and put your writer's anatomy to work.

Writing is like any other career. Learning and practice help you become really good at something you love. Visualizing yourself as a writer and pounding out words, sends messages to brain cells that specialize in that area. Has an idea ever magically popped into your head? That's your instinct kicking in and answering your plea for an idea.

Your brain operates on the roadmap you provide. Putting out the word that you want to be a writer puts your brain into motion. In turn, it sends juicy ideas, strings together delectable sentences that take you by surprise, and moves you in the direction of a completed article proposal. It could just as easily send you to the grocery store for eggs, gambling on the stock market, or tell you how to build a bridge. Your brain doesn't randomly send you on a wild goose chase without having a little help from your thoughts and actions.

Brain cells that nurture creativity and writing need proper exercise and nutrition. There are more brain cells than we realize working diligently behind the scenes to nurture writing dreams into reality. Some brain cells help us put words to paper despite our fears and doubts. Others keep us organized, help us conduct research, or edit our writing. Brain cells transform scattered ideas and words into articles and stories that have the power to make readers laugh, cry, cheer, or consider life from a different angle.

Writers, like athletes, need a workout routine to maintain a healthy, creative anatomy. Athletes cross finish lines because they work hard, exercise and feed every muscle. Starting out, they may have some understanding as to 'what' needs to be done, but may not know 'how' to go about it. That's why they have coaches and trainers. Consider me your coach and this book a training manual for helping you become a high-performance writing athlete.

Many good books I read on freelancing covered the 'what', but not enough of the nitty, gritty 'how'. My willingness to get my hands dirty and figure out 'how' to give editors, readers, and clients what they needed and wanted contributed greatly to my publishing and corporate success throughout the past 15 years. I leave nothing out. From idea conception to cheque in hand, I not only give you detailed instructions, but also provide full illustrations of everything to expect. This is the real deal.

Chapter 2 - Starting Out

Fear had kept my writing hidden in desk drawers. Leaving my three-year old daughter to work full-time after divorcing became a greater fear that motivated me to brave the publishing world. After the divorce, she needed me to help her feel safe and secure. Writing is in my blood and has been since I was four years old. Bringing it out into the light helped me become a better person and mother.

I can see myself pushing her on the swings, making snow pigs together, or re-enacting Bambi. We wore out board games and loved cuddling together and reading. Working in the middle of the night, or before the sun came up gave me time during the day so I could share in those precious memories. It left me weary at times, but with no regrets. Bumpy roads many times have the best views.

Fear lines many dreams. As a child I felt no fear, just this inexplicable burning desire to write. The stories that moved others in the same way I'd been moved when reading Heidi, Little Women, and the Black Stallion. But what if I started to write and the words didn't come or worse, were absolute crap? What if everyone else was right and I should get a 'real' job as an accountant, secretary, or lawyer? Everyone had a different opinion. Our fears and those of others turn life's little baby steps into thundering, giant steps.

Operating my writing dream as a business stripped away the romantic notions, put me to work, and helped me dispel irrational fears associated with writing. I needed to learn how to work as hard for myself as I had worked for total strangers in the corporate world. I created work plans, schedules, and rules to keep me writing. Rules like, your desk is your office. Show up on time and work hard. Clean your desk at the end of the day. Keep and eat all snacks at your desk so you don't wander off into the kitchen and forget to come back. Most importantly, never forget to commend your hard work.

Fear left to run wild acts like a rogue cell that disrupts healthy, working cells. When real and present danger exists, true instinctive fear kicks in and screams things like, "Don't go down that alley! Don't touch that hot stove!"

Imagined fear born from doubt and believing in the worst possible outcome sounds like a whiney, critical back seat driver. It says things like, "I don't think your mom would approve. Do you really know what you're doing? Can we just eat ice cream and lay on the couch instead?"

I can still see the relieved look on the student's faces in my writing class when I told them how my hands shook when pushing my first proposal out the door. Fear as I've learned is a dramatic actor, but not a character flaw. Sometimes it's the laid back dad, sitting in his shorts, with one eye on the television who says, "Sure honey. Go ahead and take the car," forgetting you don't know how to drive. Other times, it's the horror movie mother who says, "We're all going to die if you leave the house." Lots of drama, but not too many bruises.

Never be embarrassed or ashamed to admit you have fears. Reassure the trembling voice inside and keep moving. You are the boss. There are still days when I roll out of bed and think today is the day words will stop flowing from my brain and onto paper. Despite these fears, I get out of bed anyway, turn on my computer, and hope for the best.

Dismissing thoughts of perfection or the perfect goal injects adventure and takes fear down a notch. Before knowing better, I considered every proposal with the weight of a life or death decision. Fear never leaves entirely. It does keep me checking and double-checking to make sure my words are wearing clean underwear before leaving the house.

Achieving a certain level of publishing success should not be a measure that determines whether *you* are a success or keep writing. Life is about learning. Always be proud when you try something new, or something scary. That in itself is a lesson and a sign of growth. Life may be easier on the sidelines, but I've found it less fulfilling. Get out of bed, out of your head, and onto paper.

After a lifetime of running to and away from being a writer, I can tell you that a belief in learning is the knight in shining armour when it comes to taking down fears. Learning and practice are the tools that equip any career life raft. Seeing writing as something I could learn, rather than a faint gene I may or may not have gave me confidence and a belief it could be done.

Unless you are dangling from a cliff, the question you need to ask is, "What do I have to lose?" Editors declining a proposal just say, "no" and I am no worse off than before I sent out the proposal. When rejection letters arrive, I simply ask, "Is there something I could have done better?" and then I get right back at it. Brain cells have great listening skills. When you send out calming, reassuring messages to fear, it puts down its gun and creativity comes out of hiding.

When I chose to unleash my writing on the world, I had many questions as to how to get ideas from my desk to an editor's desk. One less than practical question I asked was, "Should I rush the ideas out the door in hopes of a quick, fluky sale?" The irrational side of me wanted to cut right to the chase and send something out. Something in my business brain and instinct said, "Bad idea." When I don't want my dog to run out in traffic, I say, "Wait." Every writer needs that word when compelled to send out a half-baked proposal. Not "wait forever," just wait for a brief moment, look both ways, and ask yourself if you did your research before letting your words cross the street.

I started writing in my head before I knew how to put words to paper. When times are tough, or I'm confused I can count on my writing. It's the rhythmic heartbeat that keeps the rest of me alive and I work hard to nourish and support this essential part of my anatomy. Write because you love to write. The likelihood of having some degree of success in anything is heightened when it's something that beats in your heart day in and day out.

When I started pitching magazines, I knew that like any other job, getting ahead meant proving myself. I tossed my beret in the closet, dropped my romantic notions, and went to work. When teaching this course, many students arrived with the same romantic notions before I put them to work. Ninety per cent (90%) of students in my classes using this program have consistently created successful query letters! Let's get started.

Chapter 3 –Writing Spaces and Places

Routines and habits are road markers that remind your brain of your destination. Setting aside specific hours to write in a designated area is the starting point that puts a brain into gear.

Brains, like other muscles, stiffen up if not exercised properly. Using different creative tactics keeps your brain from getting in a rut and stiff. Unless you find it productive, don't try and force your brain into a boring routine where it comes to believe that writing is something to endure rather than enjoy.

Sometimes, my brain likes complete quiet. Other times, it likes the soothing sounds of nature, or country music. Be a great host to your creativity and serve it delicious, stimulating treats.

Sitting in the same position stiffens up not just your brain, but also your back and hips as well. Switch it up. Stand, sit, lie down and most importantly, **stretch**! Do whatever it takes to keep writing.

I also have a rescue place at the Banff Performing Arts Centre for the times when I feel blocked or frustrated. Staring at the mountains through the huge bank of windows while writing works every time.

Please do not go out and spend hundreds or thousands of dollars on a workspace. You don't need an office or special furniture. They can be any shape or size. A friend I once mentored completely derailed her writing before getting started for this very reason. Upon asking her to show me her first draft, she said, "I've been so busy, painting my work space, buying furniture and supplies that I haven't done any writing." She then proceeded to tell me that she needed to get a part-time job to pay off the debt.

Like a conductor raising his baton to signal the start of a symphony, writing spaces signal your brain to commence writing. Teach your writing brain to become a creature of habit.

Assignment: Take one afternoon to setup or designate your favorite writing spaces and places.

Chapter 4 - Anatomy of a Magazine

Why research a magazine?

I can handle most challenges provided I'm taking some kind of concrete action. While I knew it needed to be done, researching didn't feel like action because in my mind it wasn't writing. In a forest, the yellow-bellied sapsucker drills holes in the trees. Like many others, I thought they drilled for bugs to eat. Turns out they drill holes not only to eat, but to create nest cavities for small song birds and release the sap for them to eat in the Spring. Everything in nature has a purpose and contributes to another species. Everything in the writing process including research has a purpose and contributes to the quality of a proposal and article. Research helps you understand a magazine's anatomy, readers and advertisers, and article structure, Research also stirs up ideas. It's your woodpecker.

Starting out, I studied the anatomy of the magazines I liked from cover to cover. Magazines provide guidelines for 'what' they want to see in a proposal. I needed to figure out 'how' to do the 'what'. For example, guidelines typically say, "Make sure your article is suitable for our publication." Determining suitability requires an understanding of a magazine's format, audience, layout, tone, and editorial calendar. In other words – research.

Work smart, not hard. Researching magazines helps you focus your efforts. The first step to increasing your odds of success is identifying magazines open to generously accepting freelance submissions and that pay well. This increases your odds of getting a proposal accepted.

In search of information on 'how' to write proposals I found more rah-rah sisboomba than substance. When instructing my *Writing for Magazines* course, graduates of prestigious journalism programs said that they learned more about pitching an article in six weeks than they had during four years at university. Many books and sometimes courses on writing provide the theory, but not enough practical detail as to 'how.'

I also found the same thing with many articles I read. Lots of 'what', not enough 'how'. Editors liked that I went a little further by providing 'how' details in my articles. I didn't want to write articles that read like introductory computer manuals that tell you how to press the power button and leave you hanging as to the rest.

Tapping into a weakness I observed in the corporate world, gave me a leg up when breaking into publishing. Many people starting a new job try to dive in without first becoming familiar with the ways in which their job ties into the objectives of the company. They don't take the time to read the company's background material and strategic objectives, or familiarize themselves with the clients they serve. I excelled in the corporate world out of my willingness to do all of those things and more. Taking shortcuts really ends up taking you way out of your way. Ask any woman driving along with a man who thinks he can find his way without a roadmap. Sorry boys.

As I began my research into freelancing, I realized that many new writers dive into the writing world without a roadmap. By familiarizing myself with a magazine's structure, content, audience, editor's expectations, and article format I walked past all of those who either didn't understand what they should be researching, or thought they didn't need to bother with the research. Learn to be the best you can be at whatever you do and you move one step closer to your goal.

Researching a magazine is no different than researching a company before sitting down for a job interview. In the beginning, I moaned at the thought of research. I wanted to play with my words, not sit in a library basement, or drown browsing the Internet. After dissecting the first magazine, I realized very quickly that the process revved up my ideas and led me down the right path. Editors repeatedly told me that my creative titles and leads, and meticulous work ethic kept them buying my articles.

Once you review and analyze a magazine a few times, it goes by faster because you've developed a keen eye for recognizing a magazine's anatomy. Be patient with the research and resist the urge to prematurely push a proposal out the door.

Beating the Odds

As a virtual unknown I sold **eight** of the first 15 proposals I sent out! Believe me when I tell you that those are amazing statistics for an unknown. When I sent a few of the rejects back out the door I managed to sell those as well.

Odds are the name of the game in sales and article proposals. Like other sales people, writers are subject to the law of odds. Keep in mind that there are many good writers pitching good products alongside you. My attention to detail, following instructions, and creativity thrust my submissions past those who had yet to learn how to research.

There are statistics on the odds of selling anything. Writers starting out with basic knowledge have on average a 15:1 chance of selling an article idea. In other words, of the 15 different proposals you send out, you have a chance of selling one of those proposals. How did I interpret those odds? I determined that by meeting editor's expectations and increasing my volume I could improve my odds of success.

On average, a direct sales person contacts 15 people to get three leads and one sale. Using the same premise in publishing, you need 15 ideas, to come up with three great angles, to publish one article. Pinning my hopes on one idea seemed as logical as my dad's horse racing theory. He always bet on the tallest, darkest horse with the longest tail. That's what you call a longshot. A longshot in writing is sending out one pitch without conducting research and then sitting and tapping your fingers while waiting for the phone to ring.

Despite the statistic, I felt convinced that I could beat the odds and I was right. Researching the industry and writing endlessly to improve my skill is how I beat the odds. Reading this book already indicates your willingness to do whatever it takes. Beating the odds is a combination of creativity, hard work, and research. It's not magic; just mechanics.

Choose Magazines First, Ideas Second

Do you want to make freelancing hard? Come up with ideas first and then try finding the right magazine audience for the idea. It sounds like it should make sense, but not really. Starting with little background knowledge is likely to sprout ideas previously published and perhaps even many times over.

After I researched and found magazines I believed suitable to my style, better ideas followed. Lots of ideas. And, they were more likely to be a fit because my research sat in the back of my mind filtering out stale ideas. Research is like a can opener that opens the lid on deep seated, truly great ideas.

As soon as the idea to write for magazines occurred to me, article ideas started trickling in, then rushing in. Where the mind goes, creativity follows. Remember, all cells within our anatomy are connected through communication. Many of my first ideas were more beans than bangers. Research steered my ideas in the right direction. Yes, the grunt work that no one wants to do. During job interviews, employers like to ask applicants what they know about the company. Successful applicants tell a company how the skills they offer can help the company achieve their objectives. Great sales presentations are built on a foundation that illustrates the ways in which a product's features benefit a company. Enthusiastically illustrating how your article idea benefits a magazine's readers is the foundation of your proposal or sales presentation.

Research magazines backwards and forwards. First, to become familiar with your target market. Secondly, to verify that your article ideas or anything similar has not been published within the magazine you are targeting or their competitors within the last two years. Editors are looking for fresh ideas, not yesterday's news.

While reviewing the magazines I wanted to target, I found a few of my so-called 'original' ideas staring back at me from the pages. That's painful. The reality is that others think alike and can get the same idea to market before you even start a proposal. At times, ideas surface from something previously read, but not forgotten. Don't slap yourself over it. In a day and age of information overload, it's easy to come up with ideas from something you read. You will find original ideas.

When breaking into the business, a friend of mine had also started freelancing. During our discussions, I mentioned an article idea regarding charter schools. A few weeks later, she mentioned that she'd sold that idea to a local magazine! My chin dropped to the floor and I replied, "I mentioned that idea to you a few weeks ago." She genuinely looked mortified. Admittedly, I did wonder if she had truly forgot its origins, but I gave her the benefit of the doubt. We ended up working on the article together, and shared the by-line. Magazines don't generally allow more than one writer to share a by-line and in this case because she had already sold the idea, my by-line read 'With Research from Louise Blank'. We agreed to no longer share ideas to prevent this from happening again and potentially damaging our friendship. I didn't become paranoid, but I did guard my ideas going forward. Thinking someone else's idea is ours, can happen. Editors, also keenly remember writers who waste their time with previously published ideas.

Authors are prolific readers who in the process, unconsciously pick up story writing techniques. Being a well-read freelancer gives you the same advantage. You pick up language, tone, rhythm and the caliber and number of sources a magazine prefers.

In a proposal, you must tell an editor why the subject appeals to readers, which magazine section and editorial calendar slot you believe is appropriate. How can you gain this knowledge without reading enough issues to understand a magazine's structure and style?

Along with structure and style, you also need to become familiar with the advertisers who keep the lights on at a magazine. Would magazines filled with makeup ads publish an article on the ethical testing of makeup? Would magazines focusing on mid-lifers be interested in tips for getting pregnant? That's an obvious one, but you get the point.

Every hour I spent researching magazines paid off in ideas and getting an editor's attention. Coming up with an idea without doing any research and trying to shoe-horn it into any magazine significantly reduces your odds of selling a proposal.

Writing for the magazines you like and read makes research easier. You have already developed a kinship with the magazines whether you realize it or not. Developing ideas and writing articles for that magazine becomes second nature. Accepting articles from consistent competent, writers makes an editor's day easier and they inevitably look for more ideas from that writer.

Bottom line – if you don't feel a connection with a magazine, editors won't feel a connection with you. Become an expert on the magazines you are targeting.

Assignment: *Based on subject matter or people that interest you, select five magazines that you believe are suitable markets for the research you will be doing according to the instructions in the following pages.*

Writer's Guidelines

Writer's guidelines, similar to a job description describe a magazine's needs, expectations, and the desired qualifications they seek in a writer (e.g., previously published). Guidelines, also describe what editors expect to see in a proposal. Until a few years ago, most magazines published writer's guidelines. Today, however, you will find fewer guidelines. If you cannot find guidelines on a magazine's web site, request them through the site's Contact page. One way or the other, they will let you know.

Magazines where guidelines are not available may have little interest in freelance submissions. Or, they may want freelancers to dig a little rather than being spoon fed information about the magazine. Many writing organizations publish reference books or lists of magazines accepting freelance submissions that will also include summary guidelines. Verify that they are current.

Significant details in the guidelines may include:

— what will, or will not be accepted in the way of genre and subject matter

— when a response to a proposal can be expected

— how to send pitches (e.g., email, submission page, snail mail)

— whether or not attachments are allowed in emails

Guidelines for formatting a proposal (e.g., spacing, details to include) follow an industry standard. The good news is that everything you need to know about submitting a proposal is in this book. Your job is to hunt down and find magazines that offer the best freelance opportunities. Cross-check every submission against the magazine's guidelines to verify that it meets all requirements.

Assignment: Obtain writer's guidelines for the five magazines you've selected. Where guidelines indicate that freelance submissions are not accepted for any of the magazines, find a replacement magazine(s) to maintain a minimum of five magazines for your research.

Articles Wearing Snowshoes in June

Believing that you have a good idea isn't enough. Beyond knowing *what* content a magazine publishes, you also need to understand *when* they publish material. Thus, the editorial calendar. Magazines plot out issues based on seasonal influences, not incredible ideas writers throw on the pile.

Article ideas may help them see a potential new way for focusing an issue, but that is an exception. More likely, they are developing the editorial calendar around seasons, advertisers, trends, and the potential for more advertisers. Advertisers influence all media forms whether they are magazines, web sites, or television and radio stations. Articles can be rejected because they don't reflect an advertiser's values. That's why you don't give up after one rejection.

Assignment: Request editorial calendars from the five magazines you are researching. Where do your ideas fit in the editorial calendars?

What's your minimum wage?

Freelancers sometimes mistakenly believe they need to approach non-paying, small publications first. Not true. I sold eight of the first 15 proposals I sent out for a $1.00 per word and without previous experience or clippings. While experience gives you credibility, so do creative leads, great writing, and illustrating to editors that you took the time and effort to familiarize yourself with the magazine and its audience.

Researching a magazine also includes looking into pay rates. From a business perspective, pay rates speak to the financial health of a magazine, maturity, and the value they place on freelancers. The rate you are willing to accept speaks to what you believe about your worth as a writer. This is very personal, and also hinges on your priorities.

My need to stay at home with my young daughter and limited available work hours meant I needed to work smart not hard. Pay rates factored greatly into my decision when submitting proposals. I determined my minimum wage needed to be no less than $1.00 per word and I sought out magazines with good reputations who were willing to pay the going rate.

The time that goes into researching, brainstorming, and editing an article goes many hours beyond the time you spend putting words to paper. In the end, your net pay that takes **all** time and supplies into consideration is quite a bit less.

Research, kickass angles, and great sources give you the confidence to pitch reputable magazines and seek the pay you deserve. When my proposals went out the door, they were testament to my effort and creativity and worth every dollar I received, if not more.

Every time I taught my writing class, someone on the first day inevitably asked, "How much will I get paid?" As much as I loved being a freelancer, it wasn't exactly the type of reliable income needed to raise my daughter on my own. Nevertheless, I determined that I could make a living with other forms of writing.

There are two questions that need to be asked when considering pay. What is good pay according to industry rates? What pay is sufficient for you to eat and pay the bills each month? Answering that question requires creating a realistic budget from actual expenses and income. Writers never want to do that, but it is part of the process.

Writer's guidelines typically do not identify payment rates. Check out reference books published by writing organizations that list freelance opportunities along with rates.

Don't Write Just for Money

Writing for money after the divorce came out of good intentions, not greed, or ego. Dollar signs kick my ego and fear into action that work like chunks of cholesterol blocking my arteries and inevitably my creativity.

Try to think of articles more as works of art and less as cash cows. That's pretty difficult in today's society where the economy is our new religion and debt looms over our heads. There are writers who choose a simple lifestyle over material possessions so they can dedicate their time to writing.

I'm not saying writers have to cast away all worldly possessions. Thinking only of money when you write, however, is kind of a creativity buzz kill. Creativity is less of a capitalist and more of a monk.

Nothing gets me into more trouble when my focus zooms in on money and ignores all else. We all need money to pay the bills. Many of us dream of having financial security so we can worry less about paying bills, and enjoy more freedom when it comes to where we live and work. When I focus on money, my thoughts sound whiney, manipulative, and conniving like a spoilt child trying to get her own way at the candy store. I stamp my feet, pound my fist on the table, and demand that someone show me the money so I can dedicate myself to writing what I want. Creativity covers its ears, turns on its heel, and fades into the background.

Avoiding money's distractive qualities can at times be difficult. Amongst the greatest lessons in my life is the one where I learned to live each day according to a vision that creates a warm, fuzzy, content feeling inside. Fulfillment is hard to describe. Becoming focused on money for any reason leads me down a muddy path, that fulfillment doesn't follow.

It's easy to get sucked into the material game once in a while. And when it happens, I reach back into my life at age four where my desire to write rose from the purest part of my being that knew nothing of celebrity or greedy desires. Once I am re-centered, I leave the rest to the universe and say, "I trust you to provide." While I have buckets of faith and belief, I'm also enough of a realist to pull up before I have no money to keep the lights on and am eating cat food! As convinced as I am that what I'm doing feels right in the moment, that doesn't always mean I always get it right.

When I walk within the context of my vision, my controlling nature dissipates. The universe loves to laugh at those of us who think we have more control. Believe in your vision, and so too will the universe.

I learned how to live my life and write from the most genuine part of my soul. My deepest desire is to make 100% of my living writing. That being said, I also learned that I need to eat, have a roof over my head and drive a comfortable car. For now, I work to support my freelance writing the same way my brother worked to support his farm. I just make sure that my corporate work always includes writing to keep my hand in the game.

When I finished school, I let others talk me into getting a 'real' job and temporarily dismissed my dream of being a writer. Being young is the time to test out your dreams, or at least get started. Considering my delayed start in writing, I have done very well. Sometimes I imagine where I would be today if I had started earlier.

Given a do-over early on, I would have listened more to my own instincts, partied less, and put relationships on hold so I could immerse myself in the craft of writing. Be brave new writers. Dedicate and immerse yourself in the craft of writing for at least five years early on to give it your best shot. You have nothing to lose but a stack of unwarranted fears. Live in a writing epicenter where you can inhale the energy and learn from the best. Create a simple lifestyle where part-time work or income from writing is sufficient to maintain a decent standard of living and keep you writing.

Then again, for others like myself, please know that it is never too late.

The desire to write needs room to breathe. Trying means learning and learning is never a waste of time. It maintains our existence. Writing isn't just about getting paid, or being published. Writing has taken me down roads I would have never explored, introduced me to experiences that left an indelible mark on my heart and gave me courage to try other things I may not have considered.

Starting earlier gives you a good handle on the process and room to seek opportunities you may not be able consider later when you start a family. Writing as a *career* is my first love. My daughter is my most important love and first priority. Knowing what I know today, there are things I would have done differently early on to give my writing career a better chance. I don't look at it with regret. It's merely a lesson learned I'm passing onto you.

When asking someone about what career they dreamed of as a child, many can't recall having a dream, but I did. More like an itch. That's how writing feels to me. No matter how many times I try drowning, starving, or running it over, it never gives up on me. It started as a thin blade of grass and grew into a rock solid oak tree that I cannot and now do not want to ever cut down. As I let it grow, it helps me grow. The best advice comes when my pen hovers over a piece of paper, or my fingers hover over a keyboard. It's the tow truck that drags out my feelings. Scratch your writing itch, but not just for the money! Love it first, sell it second.

How Magazines Pay

Payment is typically per word in the magazine world. I vowed that I would never write for less than a $1.00 a word. The rate typically varies based on the publication's readership and advertising revenue. It can start at .10 per word and go as high as $3.00 per word.

Most writers start out with small pieces in the Upfront sections of magazines. Unfortunately, advertising is slowly edging out small articles. Upfront sections and short articles provide springboard opportunities for new freelancers. They serve as a stage where editors test a writer's aim with small game before assigning you big game. The awesome thing is a freelancer's work is what readers see first in the magazine! Think about that for a moment.

It takes many 250 – 400 word pieces to pay the bills. Some writers love short pieces because of the variety and fast pace, and end up making a modest or part-time income. There is nothing wrong with doing volume, but you still must consider the odds.

With our attention span waning, article length is getting smaller by the year. There are few 3,000-word full-length features. Full-length articles are more likely 1,200 – 2,000 words. In-house writers, editors, or stringers, many times write two-thirds of a magazine's feature articles. In a day and age of celebrity fascination, many features profile celebrities rather than everyday people that are making a difference or overcoming challenges.

Earning the respect and trust of an editor is no different than earning your stripes with any other boss. They need to know you can do the job before letting you dip your feet into feature writing, providing they are not pushing aside a long-time writer with a significant following. That is why you don't bet on just one editor. Groom relationships with at least 3 – 5 editors.

Industry Rates

Professional writing organizations and unions work diligently to get writers fair pay. Settling for significantly less than industry rates, impacts everyone and undercuts fellow writers. "You don't need to give away the farm," as my mother said.

For the most part, freelance rates have not increased in the past 20 years. Sad, but true. I also understand, however, the challenges magazines and newspapers face competing against the Internet's free information glut. To survive, magazines shrunk in size, articles became shorter while advertising space increased. Increases in advertising over the last 30 years is also testament to the 'consumer' society we've become.

The Periodical Writer's Association of Canada (www.writers.ca) provides an excellent rate chart that lists both technical and freelance writing rates for everything you can imagine.

According to Service Canada (www.servicecanada.gc.ca) the average full-time Canadian writer earned $44,515 in 2011. During the same period, part-time writers earned $24,215. It's important to note that these figures are not exclusive to magazine writers. This included writers of every genre (e.g., playwrights, technical, etc.).

The United States Bureau of Labour Statistics (www.bls.gov) reported median earnings of $58,850 in 2014 for full-time writers and authors. They indicate 136,500 employed writers as of May 2014 with projected job growth estimated at 2% between 2014 and 2024.

Keep in mind that figures included in government statistics, only reference 'employee' statistics and do not include annual freelancer or contractor incomes.

Here are some things to keep in mind when considering earnings as a writer:

• Increase what you earn by increasing volume and taking advantage of other creative opportunities.

• Write for free only when you genuinely want to, not because you don't believe in your writing or worth.

• Set a goal as to the minimum per word rate you will accept.

- Write for magazines with solid reputations and that pay you promptly.

Assignment: Create a personal budget and calculate the income you need to cover your monthly living expenses. Determine what that could look like in terms of writing projects and regular pay.

Cover Page – Laws of Attraction

The cover page tells you concisely who the magazine is trying to grab at the grocery checkout and reflects the season. The magazine issue used here as an example illustrates the March issue's contents. Spring reflects a time of hope, renewal, and cleaning. Article titles appearing on a cover page reflect topics relatable to Spring and a target audience of on-the-go women aged 25 – 45. Article captions on the cover page included:

- Household organization

- Easy weekend dinner plans

- In defence of laziness

Assignment: Select one magazine cover and based on the article captions, determine what readers you believe are the target audience.

Contents Page – How A Magazine is Organized

The Contents page illustrates how articles in the magazine are grouped and prioritized. The magazine layout focuses on maintaining reader interest and drawing them to the ads. Editors might hate to hear that I read magazines from back to front.

Below is a summary of what I found when researching the magazine I'm using for illustration purposes. The sections are fairly typical of what you might find in a lifestyle magazine.

In Every Issue – editor's letter at the front and a celebrity interview, column or essay at the back

Notebook – this is comparable to an Upfront section. The issue focused on the arts. There are four articles approximately 800 words in length profiling artists and writers. This suggests the growing trend of single, professional women connecting with the arts.

Assignment: *For the five magazines you are using for research, identify current trends for each magazine's target demographic. Where could you find interesting people to profile that are movers and shakers amongst the trends?*

Style – mostly soft advertising for cosmetic products and fashion reviews anchored by additional ads and short 250-word pieces. Style sections are typically written by in-house editors.

Home –this section offers articles and advice on home organization while recommending products and includes an 800-word interview with a family on how they reorganized their home. More photographs are included than narrative. The magazine's in-house design editor wrote most of the content pertaining to products and techniques. Potential for breaking into a section like this means finding a family who has unique decorating ideas or who completed a gob-smacking renovation.

Health –the short paragraph on the first page covers the benefits of outdoor exercise and includes a picture of a skier on the mount. The next page provides details on where to purchase the best ski gear.

The health column included an article on memory loss. This article targets the secondary audience (parents) related to the target audience. Not only should you take into consideration the target audience, but secondary audiences of concern to the primary audience. Middle-aged children caring for parents is a growing trend.

Assignment: *What are potential secondary audiences for the target demographic you identified in your magazine research?*

Mid-size feature (1,200 words) *In defence of laziness* provides suggestions for slowing down.

Full-length feature addresses childless women under 35 interested in information pertaining to tubal litigation. Again, this speaks to the single, working woman demographic. Being the largest feature at 2,500 words reinforces that belief and what the magazine also believes is a primary concern for its readers.

Life – profiles a volunteer doctor, finance advisor, and a journalist who recently published his book *All the Single Ladies*. Two of the three articles profiled men. Not all women's magazines exclusively profile women and men's magazines may not exclusively profile men. Keep this in mind when strategizing ideas.

Food – fast, simple cooking – one-pot meals and dishes with few ingredients and ways to use leftovers.

Every section reflects what the magazine believes are the needs of the target audience. The primary audience in this case are single, professional, women, or women married without children.

Assignment: Using the guidance I provided above regarding my assessment of each magazine section, review the sections in your five magazines. Make notes as to your conclusions regarding the target demographic and their perceived needs based on the articles and advertisers.

Masthead – Who Manages the Magazine

Typically, editors assigned to each section are identified in the masthead. This helps when addressing a section editor in your proposal. Also included in the masthead are the names and titles of other department staff and their contact information.

The masthead reveals a few things about the magazine including financial health. A magazine with only an Editor-in-Chief indicates a smaller budget. This can be either a good, or bad thing. Overwhelmed editors may be more open to freelancers. On the other hand, the magazine may not be able to afford freelancers, and the editor does it all. Many small town newspapers and local magazines work in this manner.

Cross-referencing article by-lines with the masthead helps you identify which articles are staff or freelance written. The name of the article's writer is identified either in the Table of Contents or in the article, below the title, or at the end of an article. Reviewing two-year's worth of back issues gives you a strong sense of any trends regarding the assignment of articles to freelancers.

Throughout key seasons, you may also find more articles written by staff editors. During seasonal holiday months including summer, they may defer to freelancers to cover off vacationing editors. Then again, editors may cover off for each other.

To increase your odds of acceptance, consider magazines where freelancers contribute to at least 30% of articles including full features. Section editors writing the majority of full-length articles, reduces your chances of being assigned a feature. In a day and age of increasing cutbacks, this is becoming more common.

On one occasion, I failed to do my research in comparing the masthead to article by-lines and did not understand the messaging in the writer's guidelines. In this particular parenting magazine, the guidelines said, "Please send us your ideas." I interpreted this as a welcome mat for freelancers and submitted a proposal. The editor thanked me for the idea which he enthusiastically told me an in-house writer would cover in a future issue. My 'bad' for only seeing what I wanted to see. "Thank you for your idea," in this case meant editors write 100% of the magazine's articles.

I apologized to the editor for misinterpreting the wording and believing they were open to freelance submissions. Given that they were not, I let him know that I would be withdrawing my proposal and submitting it elsewhere. I also suggested that I hoped they would reconsider the opportunity of adding robust freelance flavour. They offered to pay me for my research, without giving me a by-line. I declined on principle.

Magazines written 100% by staffers are those that may well send you a response that says, "Thank you for your idea," and then run with it. While not ethical, ideas are not copyright protected. The magazines in my opinion that do this are few. There are more details regarding copyright further on in the book.

Assignment: Cross-reference names in article by-lines to the Masthead and identify articles written by staff writers, editors and contributing editors. Based on this information calculate the per cent available in that magazine to freelancers. For example, if staff and editors wrote 15 of the 30 articles in the magazine, (.015 ÷ .030= .5) 50%, then 50% of the magazine may also be open to freelancers.

Advertisers – *Who Pays the Bills*

Advertisers are a magazine's bread and butter and the prime reason they survive unless they have millions of subscribers, or are government funded. One subscriber is worth $5 – 7. Advertisers bring in hundreds of thousands of dollars, keep a magazine's lights on, and inevitably, provide freelance opportunities. This is particularly true for magazines targeting small, local audiences.

Make no mistake, when push comes to shove, a magazine will always choose the advertiser's best interests. Never overlook this point. No matter how golden an idea may seem, or the difference you think it could make in the world, advertisers come first. For the last several years, this has posed an ethical dilemma amongst journalists. Thankfully, there are still media outlets that go against the grain and write those important articles despite advertisers.

Dairy advertisers with a full-page ad, may not be happy with an article on the adjacent page on lactose intolerance. They might however, welcome an article describing the heart benefits of Vitamin K contained in soft cheese.

You have to see beyond the idea and look at all elements of a magazine. That's the reality. Advertisers become a magazine's client based on the target demographic or audience indicated in the magazine's marketing/media package. The package is a great supplement to magazine research, but not a replacement. Studying magazines is an education that deepens your skills and industry knowledge. Looking at ads quickly helps you to identify the target audience. A symbiotic relationship exists between the magazine and the advertisers.

Few magazines can be all things to all people, which is why they target the interests of a specific age group, income bracket, gender, etc. The target demographic focuses a magazine's planning in acquiring readers and advertisers.

When first starting your research, request the magazine's media kit or marketing package that describes in detail the target demographic. Once you become good at your research, you will quickly recognize the audience after a few pages. Bottom line - writers want to find a good fit for articles and advertisers want a good fit for ads. Refer only to the target demographic in your proposal and not the advertisers when explaining why the proposal is a good fit for the magazine.

Below I have noted what I discovered when researching ads in the example magazine I'm using for illustration throughout this book:

• Three pages of advertising follow the Contents page which is then followed by the editor's note, where an ad is placed below the note.

• After the editor's note there is a 'Style Notes' page that references name brand products.

• Two additional full-page ads followed the style notes and those products were also included in the 2015 Beauty List – in other words, soft advertising. Magazines may not agree, but in my opinion, this is an advertorial.

• Of the 131 pages in the magazine, 50 pages included full-page ads. In other words, advertising took up 38% of the magazine.

Assignment: Using the magazines you selected for your research, identify the core advertiser type (e.g., fashion finance, health, etc.) and how many pages, or what percentage of the magazine (number of ad pages ÷ by total pages = per cent of ad pages) is dedicated to advertisers. What articles do you believe are compatible with the advertisers and which are not? How do they pair advertisements with articles?

Editor's Note – Tone from the Top

The editor's note provides a personal reflection from the editor on the issue's focus. This strategy invites readers to also consider their personal connection to the articles. The note can also hint at an editor's likes and dislikes. Consider the editor-in-chief as the head chef who sets the magazine layout the same way a chef develops a menu. Section editors are the assistant chefs who determine the ingredients needed for the magazine's appetizers and entrées.

Editor's notes on personal experiences inspired a couple of my ideas. Where appropriate, a proposal can relate back to an editor's comment and how it led to your idea. This connects the editor to your proposal. It also shows that you took the time to read the magazine and gain an understanding of its audience and objectives before submitting a proposal.

The editor sits at the big table when it comes to giving the finally blessing for your proposal. Pay close attention to the editor's note as they are telling you about their passions and pet peeves. Note the editor's tone, language, and tempo all of which continue to dapple the pages throughout the magazine. Sprinkling some of that flavour in your proposal shows again that you researched the magazine.

Assignment: Read the Editor's Notes in the five magazines you are researching. Make notes of the tone, likes, dislikes and potential ideas that come to mind.

Final Notes on Research

Some of you are probably getting the wrong idea and think that this means you can't write your dream articles. Your first ideas may in fact be dead on and successful. I am only suggesting that research puts the final touches on good idea and takes it from good to simply fabulous!

I guarantee however, that somewhere in this process, knock-your-socks-off ideas will rise to the surface. Count on your writer's instinct becoming sharper with every magazine you research, every idea you develop into an angle, and every pitch that tells an editor exactly why it fits the magazine.

The practical mechanics I offer you in this book are those that helped me gain more business and professionalism in the front and less writer's romanticism in the back.

Research as I have learned can be addictive and lead to procrastination if not careful. While valuable, excess research hours chip away at the writing and editing hours needed to fully-cook a proposal. Time management is critical. With a toddler running around my legs, I had to be especially careful about scheduling. We all know how minutes can lead to endless hours when browsing the Internet.

Every minute spent doing unnecessary 'make busy' work takes away from minutes you could be writing. Browsing drains my energy the same as television. Allocate research time into your schedule and stick to that amount of time. Setting an alarm helps. Don't give into the temptation to spend five more minutes. When you're done, be done.

Chapter 5 - Geography and Specialty Advantage

Geography

Every day, many things occur within our anatomy that go unnoticed, or are taken for granted. Within a magazine's anatomy, there are subtle hints within the pages that point to other ways of selling your ideas.

Much like the U.S., Canada's publishing world primarily lives out east. This presents a challenge for national magazines that want to reach audiences across the country. Living in Western Canada gives me the unique advantage of being closer to the pulse of western living and sources. When I started out, national magazines were desperate for articles about the people, places, and things happening out west so they could attract western readers.

In countries with a diverse population, magazines are now offering not only national coverage, but also global coverage related to varying cultures. Unfortunately, in some instances it's diminishing local content. Magazines are trying to connect with readers through cultural traditions that serve as a lens for how they perceive and react to the world.

The Internet has increased the reach and access to audiences around the world. Nothing however, beats a local writer with an ear to the ground who can better authenticate facts in person at that locale.

Look for geographical opportunities in a magazine. However, this doesn't mean that a magazine focused on Maine life wants articles from Calgary. They may however want articles regarding lifestyle trends that could affect Maine residents.

Hot topics trending in your city or town may be important, or on the horizon for other places. Read small town newspapers. Depending on the topic, small town news can be important nationally. Tell the stories of local heroes, influencers, and innovators.

Friends or family from other geographical areas can be great sources for ideas. My visits home to Winnipeg, have triggered many a successful article idea.

Assignment: Review a magazine that targets a national audience and see if you can find a geographical gap in the content. Using the suggestions in the section above, come up with three ideas that leverage the geographical advantage.

Specialty

Developing a specialty is similar to being a columnist in that you offer expertise in a particular area. As a specialist, you have eyes on everything relevant to the specialty including a reliable pool of expert sources who can also keep you informed regarding that industry's trends. There are no boundaries except you may want to focus on a specialty within topics that have mass appeal such as health, travel, food, gardening, business, finance, education, parenting, fashion, etc. Focus on a specialty within a specialty, and come up with unique angles rather than generalizing.

Gardening became one of my specialities that resulted in several articles and a book. Being from a windy, mountainous location, I proposed innovative ideas for keeping soil warm at night and strategic placement of plants and flowers that needed soil that stayed warm overnight. The idea came from trying to overcome that challenge in my garden and not finding any solutions.

On another occasion while touring gardens, I noticed that many people only grew roses amongst other roses. In my own garden, I'd created wonderful displays of colour and texture, by pairing roses with other plants and flowers. The concept resulted in a published article with pictures at the ready.

Developing a specialty leads you by the nose to ideas. Becoming a specialist also requires networking and staying connected to the 'who, what, where and when' of your specialty. These connections not only foster relationships with sources, but also put you in touch with potential freelance writing opportunities within that organization. Being a published writer gave me a lot of credibility in the business world. Who knows best how to deliver a message or grab the media's attention than a journalist?

Networking with sources is happy hour for creativity and ideas, but stay within the limit. Like research, guard against too much networking and not enough writing.

***Assignment**: What do you find interesting? What peaks your curiosity? Do you have a hobby, special interest, or belong to on organization? For the magazines you are researching, do you see any gaps in specialty areas? How could your ideas fill those gaps?*

Chapter 6 - Essay vs. Article

The Essay

In the freelance writing class I taught, 90% of the students inevitably came to the first class believing articles entailed writing accounts of first person experiences. By researching magazines as suggested in this book, they quickly realized the difference. The misunderstanding came from not realizing that profiles in magazines are written by writers and not the person in the profile. Students slumped into their seats upon learning that fewer markets exist for essays and the level of effort they would have to exert when researching and writing winning proposals and articles. Their chins bobbed back up from the floor once they felt the thrill of chasing down an article idea and saw the increased opportunities.

Internet blogs are all about first person stories or commentaries. Newspaper op-ed sections provide opportunities for mostly unpaid commentaries or 'opinion' pieces that could possible get the attention of an editor.

Essays written from a personal perspective are easier to write because you are expressing an opinion and not conducting research or looking for sources that magazine articles require. They are stories you know well and have been writing in your head for years.

Successful essay writing, however, means upping your game and being not just good, but damn good at storytelling. I appreciate the storytelling, passion, and humour found in good essays. As with fiction, I like essays that bring characters to life in my imagination. Readers want to connect with someone's story.

In a day and age where more people are interested in other's lives, personal essays have gained somewhat in popularity. As with articles, the topic in an essay must also have a broad appeal rather than affect only one in a million people.

In a newspaper or magazine issue, you may find one essay which is likely written by a popular personality or expert, amongst the many other articles.

As an essay writer, you are swimming in a very large pool. Despite what you may think, many others in the pool share similar experiences. When we write about something personal, rejection feels very personal. Don't' stop writing about your personal experiences. Therapy doesn't get any cheaper. But, if you want to write articles for a magazine then keep reading. I'll leave the essay for another book. Personal experiences can be the fodder for other ideas when you look at them from a different angle. Use and abuse them to squeeze out article and story ideas.

The Article

Put aside any disappointment you have about essay writing and hear what I have to say about articles that can be equally rewarding. The successful in-depth article always profiles a 'somebody'. Readers want to snuggle up with a warm body. They want someone to validate their feelings and be able to say, "Hey! That happened to me too." Then they search for a glimmer of advice to help lighten the load.

Whether an essay or article, readers want to laugh and they want to cry. They want to learn. They want to be inspired, or motivated by someone's courage or spectacular creation. They want to be entertained and to cheer for an underdog. And sometimes they just want to escape into another's life. Magazines sit on tables in doctor's offices for a reason.

Assignment: Review three of your ideas and determine if they are essays or articles. How could you transform essay ideas into objective articles?

Chapter 7 - Ideas

Initially I thought my ideas were gold. I call this writer's protection. Who would keep going if they thought they stunk? Thinking we're fabulous keeps us going. Instructors not understanding this can quickly dash a less-than-confident writer's dream. I will refer you to my Grade 10 English teacher who slammed down a big red 'C' on what I believed to be a masterpiece. My university sociology professor helped me recover. Not having studied or prepared for my exam I had to pull a rabbit out of my ass to pass, so I went into creative writer mode. His note on my returned exam said, "For missing the answer by a mile in your essay I should give you an F. But what a great story! You made me laugh out loud, and at times brought me close to tears so I'm passing you with a C+". The moral of that story is keep swinging even when unsure and that goes for ideas.

Some of my first ideas were gold and as with most writers starting out, some were already in print. Initially, I judged my worn ideas harshly. Then I rewarded myself for doing the research that helped keep already published ideas from hitting an editor's desk and making their eyes roll. Researching magazines helped me develop a sense of well-worn ideas but also trends that opened the door to better ideas.

Like tilling a garden and churning up seeds, researching magazine markets brings other ideas to the surface. The same holds true when I wash dishes. Sinking my hands into soapy water always rewards me with inspiration. Short bursts of distraction let our sneaky creative mind slip into our consciousness. Creativity is always available. Distractions such as dishwashing, silence a busy mind so it can be heard.

Where to find ideas

The real question is, "Where can't you find ideas?" They are everywhere. They follow along during daily routines, or when you interact with others. They slip into consciousness while mindlessly observing and taking in other's conversations. They popup while you roam with friends, sit at a bus stop, sip cappuccino in a coffee shop, or lounge at a mall. Well-tuned ears and keen eyes are tracking devices for ideas.

When Barbara Frum, a noted CBC journalist passed away, they interviewed her daughter who lovingly remembered her mother as a dedicated journalist and avid eavesdropper. Journalists are perpetual eavesdroppers with insatiable curiosity and are constantly in search of a story. They sniff around for ideas the way a dog looks for a bone.

When you believe that ideas live everywhere, you can't turn around without seeing one. They appear at work, where you live, where you laugh, and where you cry. The things that bug you, make your day easier, or harder, most times have a solution and the potential for an article. Driving, in the shower, on the toilet, or lying in bed staring at the ceiling, this little voice whispers in my ear, "Write about this." Right and left of you each day are ideas waiting to be breathed into publication. Living, breathing this craft hones your writer's instinct. It's the way of our anatomy.

Researching magazines whistle for ideas to come running. After an afternoon of research, your creativity will brim with ideas and every idea holds the potential for three more ideas.

The Idea Stink Test

Being too close or attached to an idea can stink up its potential to become an objective piece. Early on, I discovered the remains of a Canadian Pacific experimental farm developed for early settlers. What I also discovered is that with the water turned off for many years the trees were slowly starving to death. Sitting on the outskirts of a bustling town, commercial developers made an irresistible offer to the new landowners. I love trees. I wanted to save the trees. I wanted to save them by article! Canadian Geographic sensing my passion for the trees declined my proposal, as the editor believed that somewhere along the line I'd lost my objectivity. I weakly tried to assure him that I could recoup my objectively, but even I couldn't convince myself let alone the editor.

While the article didn't make it into Canadian Geographic, it did appear in the local newspaper and contributed to drawing attention to the preservation efforts. People picked up and grew seedlings. A donor moved the house to another site. And, the commercial builder left the crab apple trees standing at the back of the property.

Passion and compassion are an integral part of our nature and work to the better good, providing they don't compromise an article's objectivity and integrity. If you are frothing at the mouth over a story, step back. Let the story simmer for a bit to see if you can regain objectivity. Keep in mind that seasoned editors are great stink testers and can smell rotting objectivity a mile away.

Ideas can either smell like a rose, or stink like a backhouse depending on the day. One of the historical gardens I researched for a guidebook had a "backhouse plant." The original owner planted the fragrant flowers to mask the vile smell emitting from the backhouse. Maybe a beautifully fragrant idea lies beneath a stinky idea.

Like gold panning, writers sift through ideas to find gold nuggets. That being said, don't try to push lukewarm ideas onto an editor. Trust me when I say that you know when you have a good idea. Great ideas create a strange and euphoric feeling that is hard to describe. For me, it feels a little like something clicking perfectly into place. Passing off a lukewarm idea feels like a really beige moment.

Stow stinkers in the slush drawer for another day where they may inspire three new ideas, or an innovative angle.

Playing with Your Ideas

Not playing with ideas is like weight lifting without first warming up. It's gonna hurt in that the minute your proposal goes out the door you feel regret in the realization that it needed more time. All the years I spent being afraid to pursue publication, made me want to push out proposals harder and faster to rail against that fear. Really good articles are the product of patience and play. Play puts energy into words, and expands them beyond what you first imagined.

Proposals should never leave the house without a little play. Keep the racehorse behind the gate until you hear the starting gun.

In a time when everything is done to the extreme, writers need to resist the temptation to rush words to market without first indulging them in a little playtime. Play can turn the formidable task of 'getting it perfect' into an experience you anticipate with the eagerness of a child being let loose in a park. More play means more time for an imagination to stretch and discover its true capabilities. In the end, the reward is an article where every word reflects effort. Words that skip off the page into the hearts and minds of readers and generate additional ideas. Go to www.techlet.ca to read my article "The Write Play Date" previously published in Writer's Digest magazine.

Writing play dates entail putting pen to paper, voice to recorder, or chalk to sidewalk. The idea is to brainstorm an idea without editing or criticism. Let ideas tumble freely from your imagination. When I gave this assignment to previous students, they looked sideways at one another as if they hadn't heard me correctly. "What do you mean?" To which I replied, "Write down every thought that comes to mind, exactly as it comes to mind, without editing." The students looked at each other with the same shock and disbelief as kids asked to play outside in the sunshine.

Even with clear-as-mud instructions to play, the request challenged students who hung onto the writer's guilt and a belief that writing should be endured, persevered, strained and above all perfect the first time. Inevitably, weary, first drafts tortured by editing and starchy criticism appeared before me instead of ideas given permission to run, play, and do cartwheels. Despite repeatedly assuring students that I absolutely, did not want to see perfect copy, they found it hard to believe. I understood how they felt.

Helping writers cast away worries and judgment so they can unleash their amazing potential gives me great satisfaction. The look that comes over a writer's face when an astonishingly, creative idea grows and expands into a harmonic proposal is unmistakable. Watery, humbled eyes say, "I did this. I finally did this." They have found the creative place that feels like home.

In our rushed world where we have come to believe life takes place in a half-hour sitcom, the ability to meander, contemplate, or consider possibilities that come from play is vanishing. And I'm not talking about taking a 15-minute recess or endlessly procrastinating. I'm talking about giving every article and story the time it needs to shine.

The writer's walk of shame awaits those who wait until the 11th hour to write a half-cooked article and waste an editor's time and ultimately their time as well. Everything can use a little playful polish. When I'm firing on all pistons, I can pop off some great stuff in a hurry. I have come to learn through the inevitable disappointment, that the spark doesn't always strike in the 11th hour. Shit happens and our creativity can be collateral damage. Creativity needs play, exercise, and encouragement. Treat it more like a child at the park and less like a workhorse.

An artist I knew said he had at least 35 pieces on the go at any given time. Partly, to let each layer of paint dry before applying the next layer, but more importantly, to achieve objectivity – a state that can only occur when one looks away for a while. Writing needs to be prepared for a play date and it prepares by resting untouched for a while.

Always rest any piece of writing before letting it out to play. Like the artist, have a few proposals in the works at all times so each one gets to rest. Looking at a well-rested piece of writing gives me renewed energy, enthusiasm and helps me find things I missed. My writing starts out dressed in greasy overalls and finishes dressed in Sunday's best.

Artists spend months building up canvasses layer by layer. Interior designers move furniture myriad times before achieving satisfaction. Writers, on the other hand, expect perfection with one fell swoop of pen to paper.

Play is the antidote to our internal editor who whispers in our ear, "Trim those sentences. Pick up those prepositions. Put away those dangling modifiers." Playtime is integral to the writing process.

Correction – playtime is the writing process. So, fire your editor and take your writing on a play date.

Your imagination may protest at the first breath of play's fresh air as it guiltily looks back at the nagging editor it left behind. Can you recall times when a friend invited you out and you dreaded the thought, but went kicking and screaming anyway? Once you tipped back that first drink and let out a laugh, you wondered why you fussed so much in the first place. Imagination works the same way. When you invite it to write, it remembers the last time you dragged it out for a night of editing, criticism and guilt trips. Learning to play heals those memories and editing wounds. After a time, positive writing experiences created through play push fear and worry further back. Pavlov's theory of positive reinforcement also works for writers.

The child within the writer is endlessly curious. Here are some suggestions for luring childlike curiosity off the perfection couch and out to play in the fresh air of your imagination.

- Strap on something childlike and silly such as Mickey Mouse ears or a goofy hat or t-shirt.

- Pack up your ideas and take them out on a picnic, or to a creative place like an arts centre. Energy amongst other creatives is contagious.

- Set out gummy bears or animal crackers.

- Contemplate with a yo-yo, or throw a nerf ball at the wall.

- Put on music that stirs your energy and imagination.

- Surround your writing area with playful things – I prefer my daughter's artwork and pictures of her looking at me with her cheeky smile.

Researching and playing with an article idea on parking lots morphed into an entirely different article. In the course of my research and discussions, I spoke with police experts on improving parking lot safety through environmental design. During that time, I also operated a resume business from my home. While watching the news one night, I recognized the accused murderer rushing from the courthouse as a new client who had been in my home the previous week! The article took on a very different angle regarding *Working Safe at Home*.

With more people working remotely and operating in-home businesses, the article's timing could not have been better according to the police and the editor of *Success* magazine. Wandering around the playground and the circumstances under my nose, brought together all of the concepts into a great article. The other article ideas regarding parking lots were the bonus. Ideas are infants and we are responsible for helping them grow and expand beyond narrow ideas.

Play is oxygen to the imagination, and the place where we abandon perfection for creativity. It is nourishment for the writer's anatomy that contributes to healthy writing. Play hard and work smart.

Developing the Angle

Like a thesis statement for students, putting kick-ass angles into words is challenging for many writers. Personally, I thrived on coming up with unique titles and angles. It tastes sweeter than chocolate fudge. But the more you write the better you get at coming up with titles and angles. Angles are bits of juicy steak that get an editor salivating about an article.

People think an editor's job is glamorous. After reading thousands of proposals, where they find more snoozers than doozers they are looking for you to light them up with something interesting.

While we all think our ideas are unique and golden, chances are someone else may have already come up with the idea, or something similar. Refrain from sending out proposals where the angle is even slightly similar to a recent article published in the magazine or its competitors within the last two years. Tuck those away and let a new angle stew in the back of your mind. There is always another angle.

Developing the angle in the beginning can feel awkward and strained. Practice you must. And practice with a light heart. When a good angle eludes me, I try luring it out by placing stray objects on the table. Nothing is out of reach. Cans of tuna, toys, old videos - simple random objects to mess with my creativity. My brain goes into WTF mode and scrambles to come up with an idea because it hates the chaos and worries I'm going to set my hair on fire if it comes up empty.

Life's potholes are filled with wisdom and angles. After finalizing my divorce, I waited to sell the house, as I believed my daughter needed the stability. When I mentioned my reasoning for waiting, the realtor said, "Believe it or not the first person most couples call when they decide to split even before calling the lawyer is usually the realtor." The article light went off in my head.

Close your eyes and imagine taking a morning drive in the country. You crest a hill and there before you is a blazing, bouncing sunrise. You quietly slip out of the car with phone in hand not wanting to lose the moment. Slowly you bring the view into focus, the camera clicks and you take a breath realizing you caught that beautiful moment. That is how I feel when an idea evolves into a kick-ass angle.

Sitting alone at a desk day in and day out will not bring about great angles. Developing and growing your skill as a writer means nourishing and exercising every part of your writer's anatomy. That includes play, reading, research, socializing, meditating, changing up where you write, and providing opportunities to meander around in your imagination. All of this, brings about harmony and rhythm that cues an imagination to effortlessly spill out ideas, angles, and sentences that make people think, laugh, or cry.

The hours I spent dissecting magazines elevated lukewarm ideas into neon flashing ideas. Attention grabbing angles come to me while distracted or relaxing. Moments spent waiting at a traffic light, sitting on the toilet at 2:00 a.m., or washing the dishes all hold the potential for digging up an angle.

Divorce stories count in the millions. Tell them to family members, friends, or your cat Timmy. The editor sat up straight at the realtor angle because as she said, "I had no idea." She also knew the article would touch readers in the same way. The section editor initially refocused the angle to covering the ways in which divorce impacts the economy. The senior editor, however, wanted to go with my original angle. Even editors need to play with an angle.

The divorce article is a good example of where I took a problem affecting 50% of married couples (the who) and profiled the experts to find out 'why' many react in this way and 'how' it impacts others.

I also love sniffing out innovative people making a difference in the lives of others, or a specific industry or craft. This includes community organizations, volunteers, entrepreneurs, artists, gardening experts, or safety specialists to mention a few. Magazines don't typically provide general coverage of an organization or person. They need a good angle. Non-profit organizations overwhelm magazines with requests for coverage of events or the organization in general.

Years ago, I wrote an article that sticks with me to this day. While visiting my sister in Winnipeg I noticed beautiful murals covering spaces that for years had served as places for gang tags and vandalism. Upon returning home, I found the school program responsible for the murals. Submitting a proposal to cover the school program and murals lacked a sharp-edged angle and would receive a "That's nice, but no thanks," response. So, I started digging. In speaking with the program's teacher, I uncovered a deeply touching story of a small group of underprivileged students who despite their challenges used their artistic talent to help another family heal.

A drive-by shooter had gunned down an innocent 13-year old boy as he walked home from school. Every day as the parents went to work they had to walk by the graffiti laden site where their son had died. The police becoming aware of the trauma the parents revisited each day, approached the program's art teacher to see if the students could paint a mural over the graffiti laden site.

I still tear up to this day when I think of this touching story. The students in this class weren't just any students. Some were homeless. Some were trying to build a life outside of gangs. Several had no coats to stay warm in Winnipeg's brutally cold winters, or a bed to sleep on, and yet they came to school every day.

Before they finished the mural, winter began to set in and they continued to paint despite having no gloves, jackets and dwindling paint that had started to freeze. Those living in the community began noticing the courageous students racing to finish the site's mural before winter. In turn, they started dropping off coats, gloves, food, and paint. Tragedy gave birth to the first mural, but the inspiration and compassion of police, the teacher, students, and the community gave life to many more sites that spoke of tragedy.

Great angles are easy to find in the places where courage and inspiration live.

Sources

Good ideas do not stand alone. They need company. As visual creatures, we need to relate to a 'someone' not just facts. Input from experts and statistics support and authenticate the message brought by a personal experience. In the divorce article, realtors and counsellors are the 'someone' who tell of their personal experiences and provide expert advice related to the angle. Personal profiles include sources or statistics when the article relates to health, finance, etc.

First person account stories typically include a minimum of three experts including a statistical source. In the beginning, I went a little weak in the knees at the thought of approaching sources who were complete strangers and identifying myself as a writer. I quickly discovered that people love to help and see their name in print. Even if not interested in being a source, the worst they can say is, "No,", or hang up on you. I also discovered six more people standing in line ready to step up.

Where do you find reputable sources?

- Newspaper or magazine articles

- Public, government, police, or historic libraries are good friends and have indexes for all kinds of things (e.g., Professional Associations)

- University and college expert lists

Use keywords such as award winning, expert, leader, in conjunction with the title or description of the source (e.g., environmentalist, researcher, realtor, etc.) you are trying to find. Wherever possible, seek out top-notch sources through professional organizations where you can validate their credentials and level of expertise. Contact association Directors and ask for their opinion as to who within the association has the most expertise on the subject matter you are researching.

Organizations are usually willing to add you to their mailing list if there is potential to gain media exposure. Receiving newsletters is an easy reach into the cookie jar for additional sources and ideas.

Hanging onto sources means never taking creative license with a quote. Quotes provided by sources during an in-person or telephone interview are likely to be perfectly eloquent. Quotes provided in writing may be awkward and stiff. The best way to find awkward or unnatural sounding wording is to read it out loud. Before I ever release any writing, I read it out loud.

Some quotes may need work so they fit into the flow of an article and sound natural. Be mindful of taking direct quotes out of context during the process. A few innocent word changes can quickly send a quote sideways and a source retracting a quote.

Magazine editors can also take quotes out of context. Always let editors know that you would like to review the final copy before publication to verify that the context remains intact. After submitting an article on the return of butler service to a local magazine, the editor replaced the butler's quote with something he hadn't provided. When I asked the editor why she had created a quote of her own she said, "I think it's more interesting." I replied, "But that's not even close to what he said which means that it is no longer a quote." As a writer, it's important to protect your sources. She agreed to an alternative way of introducing her suggestions without putting the words into the butler's mouth.

Sources provide credibility and if treated well, may also bring future ideas. Misquote a source and they are gone and will encourage their associates to keep a safe distance.

In the beginning, I had university sources hanging up on me. Why? They said they were sick and tired of receiving endless requests and then being misquoted. The Chicago Tribune conducted a survey of sources where 60% said they had been misquoted. I found that outrageous and vowed I would never violate a source's trust.

How did I do this? I faxed or emailed the source's quote for them to review and sign. I let them know that I had edited the quote where necessary to align it with the article's tone. I requested sources **only** verify that the quote remained accurate and in context after being edited.

Editors and fact checkers loved this process because it reduced their workload. They went out of their way to call and share their appreciation for how my process safeguarded the integrity of the article and their magazine. Even with small articles, I provided at least three sources to reassure them of my research.

Time is never wasted building relationships and credibility with sources. With the divorce article, I queried the organizations below for sources who could provide additional information regarding the angle. Editors interested in the article will ask about sources before committing to an article.

- Canadian and Alberta Real Estate Associations to identify expert realtors

- Canadian Mortgage and Housing Corporation and Statistics Canada for real estate and divorce statistics

- One Parent Families Association and Jewish Family Services to identify counselors specializing in divorce issues

- University of Calgary Law Department for information regarding legal implications of selling a home during separation and divorce

While I didn't use all the sources, for this article, I did however, have my foot in the door with sources that could be beneficial in the future.

Protect your reputation by obtaining authentic statistics or facts from original sources. Secondary sources such as Wikipedia, web sites, newspaper articles, etc. may not be accurate or current.

Chapter 8 - Drafting a Proposal

Proposing an article or book to an editor or agent is a little like proposing marriage. You feel like you should get down on bended knee and shake with terror at the thought of rejection. The duel between dreams and fear is never ending. The unknown, rejection, and even the thought of success can rouse the inner bearer of bad news. When first stepping into the freelance ring I knew little to nothing about proposing an idea to an editor or agent. Selling a proposal is the same whether you are on bended knee to an editor or agent. You can hold out the Hope diamond (*Le Bijou du Roi* "the King's Jewel") but if you can't sell it in the first two sentences it will look like cubic zirconia to the editor.

The one-page proposal is a condensed version of the article. Queries vary in size and content depending on the article size. The average query is approximately 250 words. Even though some articles are only 250 words, editors may still want a query rather than the full article. Unless otherwise stated in the writer's guidelines, submit queries, not articles regardless of size.

When I became a regular contributor, editors no longer needed my bio and accepted 2 – 3 ideas at once in an email and sometimes over the phone. They will let you know when they are comfortable with that process.

Editors buying proposals aren't looking for a brand new version of an article. They expect you to provide an expanded version of the accepted proposal. Deliver something else and editors have the option to cut the article from the editorial lineup.

Title

Sometimes titles pop into my head first, and at other times they pop into my head as I poke around with the idea. Titles sing in the background as you develop an idea into the angle and write the proposal. As each title sings out, I write it down and then look at all of the ideas (usually around 10) together. When I'm ready to find the one that is in tune with the article. The title like the idea needs play.

Word associations, a thesaurus, song, book, or movie titles all help to stretch an imagination.

Tone

What tone resonates in your articles? Writers can be as out of tune as someone singing on stage. Did you know that no two artists have the same brush stroke? The same holds true for writers. When it comes to tone and voice each writer is unique. Tone and voice form a writer's trademark or brand. Readers who love your brand keep coming back and expect consistency whether it's an article, story, blog, or book.

Editors can sense a writer is not true to their own voice. Writing from your own voice creates rhythm in an article. Believe in, and stay true to your voice. You won't ever sound better or true trying to write like someone else.

In a magazine, your article is sings in a choir and editors would prefer that it sings in harmony. They want readers to roll gently through a magazine rather than feeling like are on a wild rollercoaster ride. Other editors, however, believe a few solo voices within a magazine can regain a reader's attention.

Newspapers, magazines, or corporate publications want writing to align with the corporate brand or tone. Editors want to hear your voice and tone in the article, providing it doesn't make the magazine sound pitchy. Maintaining your unique tone, while being within range of the magazine's overall tone is a fine balance.

Tone should also appropriately reflect subject matter. An article profiling someone working through a serious illness shouldn't sound like it's been written by a cheerleader. A light article on a fun community event shouldn't be delivered in the voice of a mourner. Small amounts of humour interjected into a heavy article can keep readers from becoming overwhelmed and is acceptable in small doses. Comedic timing is everything.

Editors have differing opinions when it comes to uniqueness in writer's voices. Some editors believe multiple voices provide diversity in a magazine and increase interest. Other editors prefer articles that flow seamlessly one after the other, as though written by one writer, and one voice. Don't be too disappointed if they rework a bit of your writing to adjust the alignment. Most magazine editors liked my strong, upbeat voice and the flavour it added to the magazine. Tone is a wild card that must remain in the forefront when you are editing as it's capable of derailing a proposal's success.

First Paragraph – Angle

Starting out, I fell into the first paragraph trap. This is where the first paragraph somehow lands in the third or fourth paragraph. I can still fall into the trap when drafting an article and that's okay providing I catch it eventually. This happens to many writers and university students writing papers. They circle around in the first two paragraphs justifying why it's a good idea. Wrong! Blast the idea right into the first paragraph. Be confident. Believe in your idea. Editors won't wait to find an idea skulking in the corner of the second or third paragraph because it's too afraid to jump up in the first paragraph.

Working in the corporate world, I conducted tests to see how many lines of an email people actually read. On average, three lines. When requesting action by a deadline, it had to go in the first line highlighted in bright yellow. A great angle grabs an editor's attention just like a sentence highlighted in bright yellow. Everything must be spelled out in the first 2 -3 sentences and peak the editor's interest because that's how long they have to grab a reader's attention. How much time do you spend checking out an article in a magazine, or reading it on the web if it doesn't grab you right away?

First paragraphs can get off to a good start with a quote, question, statistic or a combination is even better. Below are some examples.

Statistic: According to Statistics Canada one out of every two marriages will end in divorce.

Editors statistically speaking like statistics. Statistics lend credibility to a proposal. In my divorce article, statistics indicated that approximately 50% of marriages ended in divorce at that time. This screams "huge audience." Blending statistics into the first paragraph is a great way to introduce an idea and highlight audience appeal.

Quote: About three years ago, when a police officer asked Tom Robert's class to create an outdoor mural in downtown Winnipeg, Roberts saw it as an "opportunity to expand the classroom walls.

Question: Are we sitting on our art?

Magazine articles don't complain or rant, they are typically solution oriented. Including the solution in the first paragraphs is very effective. The example below illustrates the difference between a problem and solution oriented approach.

Problem Approach: Divorcing couples put up a 'For Sale' sign on the front lawn before calling anyone else. This doesn't take children into consideration.

Solution Approach: Who do people call if their marriage is in trouble? Divorcing couples are more likely to call a realtor than a marriage counsellor. Realtors, lawyers, and marriage counsellors say there are good reasons to think twice.

The first paragraph also includes the 'who, what, where, when and why'.

Who: Every article needs a 'somebody'. Divorcing couples were my 'somebody' that the sources addressed. Features usually profile a first-person account with supporting statistics or validation from sources. For example, if a story is about a person affected by a medical disorder, medical experts contribute statistics, recommended treatments, side effects or other supporting or disputing information.

What is the article's focus? Who's doing what?

Where the 'what' is taking place, or where the 'who' lives. This is very important information on a few levels. Geography can either narrow or broaden an audience. It can also narrow the target market.

'Where' is not only specific to geography in the sense of location, but also community populations dominated by nationality or religious denomination, or communities with a cultural, industrial or business focus.

When refers to the timeframe in which something happened or is going to happen. Propose events taking place in the future 3 – 6 months in advance of the appropriate editorial calendar slot. Consider the significance and comparability of other events coinciding when proposing an event.

Why is the reason an article is important to a magazine's readers? This typically involves the solution offered in the article. In the divorce article, sources suggest readers consider the impact of prematurely selling a home during a divorce vs. the benefits of waiting to sell the home.

Second Paragraph

The second paragraph provides high -level details as to the type of information sources will provide to substantiate the article's facts and angle. The first few proposals I submitted included very specific details regarding my sources which resulted in the proposals being accepted.

After a stringer at the world-renowned magazine scooped an exclusive story and source, I provided less specifics regarding sources. Details of this story and what can or cannot, be done to protect sources is included in the Copyright section. I do want to say, however, that overall, I believe most editors are ethical and support the growth of freelancers.

When working with a magazine for the first time, I only reference the type of source (e.g., award winning realtors, legal sources) and do not include names or contact information. I also let them know that upon acceptance of the proposal I will provide specific details pertaining to sources.

Referencing sources can look like this:

- . . <source type> provides answers to concerns about <topic>

- . . .the <association> provides accurate and reliable <type of information>

- . . . <source> awarded the <name of award> will provide information and statistics on <type of information>

Below are examples of how I would reference sources without providing names or contact information:

"Marital strife and divorce are responsible for the bulk of my real estate listings," says Calgary's top realtor. Real estate industry associations, banks, and housing insurance corporations say all anecdotal evidence indicates divorce as the #1 cause of market turnover, mortgage defaults and foreclosures.

Counsellors and legal professionals will provide insight into why couples may think buying a new home solves marriage problems.

Top environmental design specialists from the U.S. and Canada share expert advice on how to stay safe while working from home.

This conservation specialist of 25 years receives requests from around the world including the Queen of Denmark for his expert opinion on preserving antiques. He will speak to your readers on how to interpret and preserve the story of beloved antiques.

Third Paragraph

The first sentence in the third paragraph reminds the editor why the article is important for readers. For example: *This article will help divorcing couples weight the pros and cons when selling their home.*

The second sentence mentions whether your research identified anything similar to your idea and where and when it was published. *During my research, I found no articles within the past two years that approached the subject of divorce from this angle.*

The last sentence includes the word count and proposes the most suitable section for the article. *Thank you for considering this 250-word article for your News and Ideas section.*

Word count can be tricky, but not a deal breaker for editors if you suggest a 3,000-word article that they assign as a 400-word article. I would suggest however, that you not propose everything as a 3,000-word piece with the idea of being paid more.

Do you remember when you were in school, trying to stretch out an essay to 1,000 words because you didn't have enough substance? Same holds true for word count in an article. Full features, like a short story have layers of information, and a beginning, middle and end. There are enough meaty facts from sources to hold a reader's interest until the end. Again, researching a magazine really helps you understand what equates to a 250-word short and a full-length feature article.

If you do not have any published clippings, end the proposal with, *"If I do not hear from you by xyz date (the period they mention in the guidelines or a date three weeks from submission), I will assume you are not interested and submit the proposal elsewhere."*

If you do have clippings, provide the link to your web site where they can view the clippings, or attach the clippings as specified in the writer's guidelines. Typically, magazines prefer clippings pasted into the body of an email, rather than by attachment due to the risk of computer viruses.

Most editors understand that freelancers need to make a living and are not offended when you provide a deadline for their response. The timelines I provided aligned with timelines mentioned in the magazine's guidelines as to when a writer could expect a reply. Proposals need to keep moving especially those that are timely in regards to events or trends. As a business person, you have deadlines and schedules to meet.

If an editor is interested, I receive a phone call sooner rather than later. In most cases, interested editors respond within a week of receiving my proposal. Keep in mind that response times also depend on how frequently a magazine publishes issues. Quarterly magazines typically respond slower. Editors respond quickly if they are concerned about losing an article and because I remind them of when I will send it on to another magazine. In my mind, this is preferable to sending out simultaneous submissions that editors like even less.

Below are examples of how to frame a respectful deadline and some of the responses I've received to these requests.

Thank you for taking the time to review this 1,200-word article for your Lifestyles section. Please let me know if you are interested in this article by (date three weeks from submission). If I do not hear from you by that time, I will assume you are not interested and submit the proposal elsewhere.

Responses I received:

- I appreciated you reminding me of when to respond as sometimes things get lost in the mounds of paperwork on my desk.

- Editor sent an email or called asking for more time to consider the query.

The only sarcastic response I received came from an agent where I submitted a book proposal. She left me the following telephone message, "Thank you for your book proposal. I'm sorry but your proposal came while I was in Europe promoting books. Seeing that I missed the deadline, I just threw it in the garbage." Her tone screamed indignation **IN BOLD CAPITALS** and told me everything I needed to know.

I called back and left her a message apologizing if I had caused offence by suggesting a deadline for a response and that I was more than willing to resubmit at her convenience. I never heard back. I also didn't get angry. I did, however ask the question I always ask when things don't turn out as I expected, "What is the lesson?" The lesson is that editors are people and have preferences when it comes to submissions. As a writer, there is nothing wrong with being politely assertive. Sometimes you get it right and sometimes you don't. There are things that go right over my head and cause me no concern, but deeply offend others. Impossible, to get it right every time.

Chapter 9 - Copyright Protection

Ideas cannot be copyright protected. After my encounter with having an exclusive source scooped, the Writer's Union suggested that I include the first page of an article with the proposal with the copyright notice. This at least indicates your familiarity with rights. The publishing world is no different than any other industry. There are those who operate to the highest ethics and some who do not. In my experience, I have only encountered three unscrupulous magazines and surprisingly they were fairly well-known magazines. I asked what I'd learned from the experiences and kept on writing. Don't ever let a few unpleasant experiences taint your passion for writing.

In this instance, I had secured an exclusive interview by going through a few channels within the organization. The article regarded an innovative measure under development for protecting large carnivores from highway death. When I made a follow-up call to the magazine the Associate Editor immediately recognized the proposal and told me they had assigned it to a writer. They had not consulted me and had ignored my indication that this was an exclusive story.

The union advised that three lawsuits were pending in court against this same magazine. My source told me that one of the magazine's writers had called and he agreed to speak with him because he assumed we were associated. I could have taken the magazine to court but the Writer's Union said that it could drag on for years and be costly. I could have asked my source to decline. In the end, I put my ego aside so that this life saving innovation could get the publicity it deserved.

I believe that what goes around, comes around. In speaking with the Managing Editor, I expressed my disappointment that a leader in the publishing world felt the need to swipe stories from freelancers. In a very roundabout way, he told me that there are lazy stringers who apparently offer perks to associates that pass on queries from freelancers. You never know. I found reputable magazines, stuck with them, and let the rest go. That's the best you can do if you want to stay in the business.

Chapter 10 - Editorial Review Process

Editors get to see some awesome ideas from hard working writers. Many more things apparently look like something a grade two student submitted. Some editors receive ideas on cocktail napkins from named writers whose sense of entitlement leads them to believe that the rules no longer apply. That is why everyone from the front desk to associate editors, stand at the sentry with a checklist for filtering the thousands of queries they receive.

Large magazines receive over a 1,000 proposals each month. Typically, they publish only 12 issues each year. Within each issue, there are approximately 10 – 15 short pieces that are between 250 and 400 words. And perhaps 3 – 5 large articles between 800 and 2,000 words. This is why they have such a stringent screening process and why you must always consider how a little extra effort can help beat the odds.

While most magazines accept proposals by email, or the web site contact page, some still request snail mail. The person opening the mail checks for a self-addressed, stamped envelope used to send you a rejection letter.

They then scan proposals for adherence to the minimum requirements outlined in the writer's guidelines and spelling errors. Not complying with the basics can stop a great idea in its tracks because it speaks to a lack experience and work ethic. In the editor's mind, this equates to more work for all staff at the magazine.

Editors may look past small oversights from new writers submitting an exclusive idea with a great angle. Do you really want to take that chance when spending just a bit more time results in submitting a polished proposal with a greater chance? Every writer, including me, at some points rushes something out the door. Rejections are opportunities to reconsider whether anything could or should be done differently before sending a proposal back out the door. Absence makes an editing eye sharper. It's amazing how differently one sees a proposal after not looking at it for a few weeks and gaining more experience from writing other proposals.

If the minimum requirements are not met, a standard rejection letter is sent by email, or returned in the self-addressed, stamped envelope you provided. No envelope? No problem. No reply. Many magazines now specify, "If you don't hear back from us within three weeks (or whatever time they specify) you can assume we are not interested.

Respect the guidelines and you get to pass the first editorial review gate.

After passing the basics test, proposals move onto the Associate Editor of the appropriate magazine section. The Associate Editor reviews the proposal's angle, sources and looks for any similarities to previously published material. If they see potential, the proposal moves forward to the section editor.

The section editor reviews the Associate Editor's comments and considers the proposal's angle, audience appeal and sources. At this point, you may receive a call for more information before the section editor presents the proposal at the weekly, editorial review meeting. Section editors and the editor-in-chief review the proposals in the context of how all the articles fit together with each other and advertising for a particular issue.

Given the length and depth to which a proposal is considered, you now have an idea as to why a magazine needs at least three weeks if not more to consider a proposal.

Chapter 11 - Getting an Assignment

The Acceptance Conversation

Don't answer the phone chewing on a sandwich as there may be an editor on the other end of the line! Although, I've had conversations with busy editors while they munched on a sandwich and it doesn't bother me in the least. We all have to eat.

Stalking your email or mailbox for an acceptance response isn't necessary. Editors buying an article call. When they call, be excited, but also be cool. Don't vomit all over them with excitement. Respecting an editor's time is the first step in building a lasting and prosperous relationship for both of you.

Magazine editors interested in a proposal, provide guidance as to the approach, word count, and contract terms. The editor may request additional information before accepting a proposal. Volume and scope of additional details varies depending on the article size (400-word article vs. 3,000-word feature).

Goodness knows I wanted to pee my pants when I sold my first article, but I remained professional until I got off the phone. Sometimes when we get excited or nervous, our mouths don't know when to shut. Don't blather on about how you waited your whole life to get the call, the darndest things your cat Mittens does, or how this call will make your ex-boyfriend Bart regret the day he walked out. Writers can say the darndest things to editors.

Be genuine, brief and to the point. Typically, I say, "I'm very glad you like the idea." Then I shut-up and listen to what they have to say and answer their questions. Before winding up the conversation, they will ask if you have any questions. Contain your questions to the assignment.

Don't interject while an editor is speaking. This is a faux pas whenever anyone is speaking. Editors repeatedly comment on the ways in which I make their life easier. Be that person. When you believe that everyone puts their pants on the same way, you're more likely to act professional, and less likely to be nervous. Putting someone like an editor on a pedestal, suggests you are less. You are worthy and wonderful and have every ability in the world to write a scathingly great article. Believe in that always.

Upsell

Upselling is everywhere, even when eating out. Order wine, and they suggest an accompanying appetizer. Order an entrée, and they suggest a salad before the meal. Once the acceptance conversation with the editor finishes, ask the editor if they have time to hear another idea. There is nothing to lose. Being on the phone with an editor is a golden opportunity so go for it!

Assignment Confirmation

The Assignment Confirmation covers the agreed upon terms related to the article. The components and typical wording in a confirmation are detailed below along with some other guidelines I've provided.

EXAMPLE FEATURES ASSIGNMENT CONFIRMATION

Date/Writer's Name/Address

Assigning Editor

Issue: April

Working Title: Divorcing Couples: Think Before Selling Home

Length: 200 words

Fee: $200

Deadline: December 2

- *Contents*: As discussed, include the fact that divorce also drives the large appliance market; stoves, washing machines, etc.

- *Manuscript*: Please submit and attach in your email a double-spaced Word document

- *Fact Checking*: Please submit a separate, carefully annotated fact checking sheet. Annotations should indicate exact sources (names, email, phone numbers) for all facts in the story. This includes personal interviews and support documents for published research. Advise fact checkers if there are any special circumstances (e.g., timing, name preference (Dan vs. Daniel) to keep in mind when contacting a given source.

- *Invoices*: Submit invoices that include the article's title, invoice #, Tax# (where applicable), and mailing address in full. Note tax expenses separately.

Only writer's that have self-employment earnings in excess of $35,000 annually, require a business or tax number. When that is the case, you are responsible for billing taxes applicable to writing earnings (e.g., GST, provincial, state) and submitting the collected tax to the government. If you earn less than $35,000 and declare your earnings from writing on a personal income tax return, you do not bill a magazine taxes.

When discussing contract terms, request approval for any expenses over 5%. Indicate expenses separately on the invoice and attach receipts. Determine whether original or scanned receipts are sufficient. Indicate on your invoice that the payment terms are net 30 days from the invoice date.

Purchasing Rights: First English print and electronic rights.

- First rights allow a magazine one-time publishing use. They also specify a language (i.e., First English) and the media (i.e., print and electronic). Writing unions and association fought a long hard fight to get magazines to pay additionally for publishing an article in both print and electronic form. Most magazines pay one fee for publication in both forms. In the case of first rights, copyright returns to the author after the article is published.

- All or exclusive rights means the author gives up all rights to republish the article anywhere. The magazine owns copyright for 50 years and can republish the article or segments of the article elsewhere. For example, they could publish a 10-year retrospective of the top 50 articles and the author would not receive payment or royalties unless specified in the contract for the original article. Wherever possible don't give away the whole cow when it comes to rights. Always attempt to negotiate one-time rights with magazines wanting to buy all rights.

- Second rights apply to previously published articles purchased by a different magazine than the one who originally purchased first rights. Typically, magazines purchasing second rights pay 50% of what they would pay for first rights. Selling second rights to another magazine is easy money.

Publishing companies may manage more than one magazine, which they commonly refer to as 'sister' magazines. In an article on elder abuse that I sold to a mainstream national magazine, one of the sister magazines targeting 50+ women purchased the second rights to the article due to the significance of the subject matter.

Smaller magazines are also open to accepting second rights. It's an easy win as the fact-checking and editing are already done.

The Rejection Conversation

The rejection conversation is one you have with yourself and not the editor. There will be no afternoon tea together while they gently pat your back. What you receive is a brief, to the point reply stating your article is not suitable for publication. What should you do if you receive a rejection letter? Jump up and down and swear at the editor for not knowing their ass from a hole in the ground? Or worse, write "F--- you," on the letter and mail it back to the editor. Sadly, that's a true story! And guess what? Editors have a blacklist that they not only keep, but also share at get-togethers with fellow editors.

The things you never say to a boss apply to editors as well. Professionalism is the best way to earn an editor's trust and keep them buying your articles.

There are rejection letters and there are rejection letters. When an idea really misses the mark, or the rules aren't followed you receive a simple one or two-liner rejection. While an editor may not consider your ideas a fit, they may however, like your style. In that case, they may say, "Thank you for your recent proposal, unfortunately, it doesn't fit our editorial lineup at this time. We look forward to hearing from you in the future."

Replies received from section editors indicate they seriously considered your proposal.

Artists of every kind are very brave people. The products artists share with the world are personal creations. Because of that, rejection feels personal, but it really is just business. Voice, tone and effort are the only personality traits that interest an editor when it comes to a proposal. Beyond voice, they want to see effort put into delivery of a creative product that rejoices readers. Effort speaks to work ethic and the quality they can expect when it comes to finishing an article as they expected and on time. Late delivery drives editors towards other writers, or get you a bump in the editorial schedule. Editors, realizing they could count on me to deliver on time, bumped up one of my articles after another writer didn't come through on time.

Choose to be proud of your work even when a proposal is not successful. Millions of people move amongst each other every day with different opinions and personal preferences. What may not appeal to one editor may appeal to another editor.

Chapter 12 - Getting Paid

Contracts are legally binding agreements identifying terms (including payment) agreed to by both the writer and magazine. If either one does not live up to the terms, the contract is subject to termination, or used to enforce terms such as payment collection. If you do not receive an assignment contract from a magazine, there is nothing wrong with you sending a contract for signature. This is something I do with corporate clients as well. Without a contract, there is no supporting documentation for payment collection or publishing rights.

Pay is either on acceptance, or on publication. An early lesson steered me away from 'pay on publication'. I poured blood, sweat and tears into an article. Before the article saw ink, the publication went out of business and the cheque out the window. My time is valuable. Preferring to write for high paying, reliable magazines with good payment policies meant I narrowed my market, but not my profit. Work smart, not hard.

Articles are a product. Any other producer demands payment within 30 days of delivery. Writers are no different from any other business.

Magazines supportive of freelancers sent my cheques within two weeks of accepting final article drafts. In turn, they received my loyalty.

When plotting out your financial planning, take into consideration the long process from pitch, to publication, and finally to payment. The time it takes to generate ideas, find sources or a someone, submit the pitch, wait for a response, write the final article, get approval and get paid can take months. Make sure you have a slush fund or alternate source of income until you have consistent and regular income.

Looking at the hard realities isn't easy. I believe people should go into the writing business with eyes wide open. Too many times, writers get pumped up with unrealistic expectations and give up on writing when inevitable disappointment comes. Writing only for money or seeing your name in print eventually leads to disappointment. It may serve as a temporary motivator, but the one thing I've discovered is that the feeling of fulfillment comes from the process of writing. The money keeps me writing but doesn't give me a feeling of fulfillment.

Everyone starting out has a few misplaced ideals. Be forgiving. Weather feelings of disappointment and keep writing.

Along with playing in a highly competitive field, the price of our lifestyle doesn't always make it affordable to write. I want to write for a living. I also want to live in a nice home. I need space. Balancing the two desires at times causes anxiety and affects my writing.

It's natural to avoid what we don't want to hear. When money is running low, the last thing I want to do is look at my bank balance, or the bills that are coming due. Facing it, as I've discovered is part of being a grownup. Pounds of emotion and passion are tied up in writing. Recognizing the realities of writing helped me become a better writer. Once I put the ugly news on the table I set out to discover how I could work around it without spoiling my love of writing, or losing my house.

Assignment: Sit down and draft a contract that includes the minimum writing rate you will accept and payment terms (on acceptance or publication).

Most magazines typically request that you send the invoice along with the article. When it comes to billing, you must be a scrupulous business operator. Never worry about annoying an editor. You deserve and should expect prompt payment. If after 30 days you have not received payment, send out a friendly reminder to the magazine's accounts payable department.

After 60 days, send another reminder and follow it up with a phone call a week later. After 90 days, it's time to involve the editor. I worked very hard to establish a relationship with the editors. Most times if the accounts payable department dragged its feet, a call to the editor lit a fire. There were also times when editors misplaced an invoice.

Difficulties with receiving payment is more likely with small magazines than with large magazines. Despite that, large magazines these days are not immune to takeovers, economic or reader downturns.

A large U.S. magazine I wrote for that had an amazing editor went out of business. The editor who valued my meticulous work made sure I received the $3,000 owed. What made it even more heartbreaking is her intent to bring me on as a stringer. I licked my wounds for a day and then let it go and kept on trucking.

In one instance, despite my friendly reminders to a local magazine, I still had yet to receive payment after 120 days. I called the publisher to express my disappointment in the poor payment policy. I also told him to expect me at his door the next morning at 10:00 to pick up the cheque. He stood humbly before me the next morning with an apology and a cheque. Respect is a two-way street for both writers and editors. Don't let the love of writing convince you otherwise. Writers contribute greatly to the success of a magazine and also deserve respect.

Assignment: Organization is key to managing stress when deadlines loom. Solid research and organization free up creativity to do its work. Draft or select an invoice template and store it in your writing tools folder.

Chapter 13 - Other Freelance Opportunities

Building a writing income can be easier if you're willing to expand your horizons. For the past 15 years, a variety of writing kept me paid and supported the writing I deeply love. Other contract opportunities included newsletters, presentations, manuals, process documentation, editing, resumes and web content to name a few.

Additionally, I self-published and sold 600 copies of a local gardening guidebook. In Canada, a book that sells 5,000 copies is considered a best seller. In those terms, I think my local book did pretty well. Always remember to give yourself a pat on the back. Never hinge your level of success on the back pats you receive from others. The measure of success is really the degree of joy and fulfillment you feel on any given day doing what you love.

While opportunities in print newspapers and magazines may be decreasing, e-zines and web sites offer additional opportunities. On any given day, you will find ads looking for writers in a variety of roles. They may want you specifically for writing social media content, web site content, or blogs. Opportunities advertised locally typically pay close to standard rates. Rates for many opportunities posted on the internet, however, are significantly below standard. Would you be willing to accept less than minimum wage elsewhere? Then, why would you accept less in the writing arena?

Corporations may need a writer for presentations, annual reports and other internal and external communications. This includes interesting profiles, press releases, and articles. While perhaps not as sexy, it makes up for it in regular pay. Once again, I will remind you to write for reputable companies and charge standard rates.

Worrying each month about how many articles I would sell, when they would pay, or if they would pay at all sent me scurrying for security. I continued to freelance parallel to my corporate work that offered a safety net. The work entailed a lot of left-brain, technical work, but it kept me writing and getting paid.

Switching back over to my right brain when I had time to write articles, stories, and books did take some effort, but eventually the wheels started turning. My creativity acquires a molasses texture when I try jockeying between left brain and right brain writing.

Writing every day exercises my imagination regardless of genre. The brain is a muscle that needs exercise. Writing is a brain's treadmill. The more I write the easier it flows. Leaving it for even three weeks is like trying to start a car left out on the street for three weeks in -30 weather. It needs a lot of encouragement and boosting. Write every day.

Assignment: *Conduct an Internet job search using keywords such as Communications Specialist, Editor, or Technical Writer. Remember to include 'jobs' at the end of the keyword search (e.g., writing jobs).*

Chapter 14 - Writer's Agoraphobia

You can't talk about writing without addressing the elephant in the room - fear. The burning desire to write is an eternal light in my life. Before finding the courage to submit my work, I filled drawers and boxes with words that never left the house. Like a paranoid mother, I kept my words from crossing the street in case they got hit by a car.

Being a creator of any kind isn't always easy in the audience of opinion. Creators are considered dreamers. I'm not the least bit ashamed. Erma Bombeck once said, "Consider boiling yourself in oil before every sharing your writing with friends and family." I have lovely supporters. Other have also rolled their eyes at my writing dreams, or told me to get a real job. These same people either picked their jaw off the floor or cried with joy to see my name attached to those first articles.

Whatever you do, do it for yourself. Do it for the feeling that fills your heart and soul when you put pen to paper, brush to canvas, or saw to wood. My dad helped me to develop a tough skin. His fatherly advice, "Do a good job because it's the right thing to do and shut the hell up. Don't bother looking for a pat on the back."

And now I'm telling you, "Go out and be the best damn writer you can be – FOR YOU."

Chapter 15 - Anatomy Review

Brain cells lounge around until they have a clear understanding of your destination which in this case is becoming a freelance writer. Now that you have read this book, you have an understanding of how your writer's anatomy works. You also have the most efficient and accurate directions for reaching your destination as a high-performance, freelance writer. Consistently following these practices will keep you from getting lost, hitting a roadblock, or getting stuck in a traffic jam.

Following the practices and routines in this book consistently, will eventually put your brain on auto-pilot. When you get out of bed, go for a walk, drive to the store, or sink your hands into a sink full of dishes and your mind will automatically switch into writing mode. Everything you need in regards to finding ideas, developing angles, and finding just the right words will slip into the seat beside you.

There is no Hemmingway gene. You have all the genes and brain cells you need. Writing, researching, brainstorming, and editing keeps your intended destination in full view of your brain's GPS.

Last Assignment: Create a to-do checklist from all the assignments in this book. Review the list every time you work on an article proposal until the process becomes automatically embedded into your routine.

Thank you for reading this important book. For additional tips and information regarding upcoming books, please go to www.techlet.ca and signup for updates. Best of hard work to you! I won't wish you luck as luck is not what get's you published.

Louise Blank's articles have appeared in major Canadian and U.S. magazines. She shared her experiences as a freelancer through articles published in Writer's Digest, Calgary Writer's Association, and the Saskatchewan Writer's Association, and in television and radio interviews with CBC Homestretch and Global television. As an instructor, she taught this course for five years and inspired many writers to believe they could indeed learn how to be successful freelancers.

Connect with me:

Web Site: www.techlet.ca

Follow me on Twitter: https://twitter.com/WriteMoreHack

Friend me on Facebook:
https://www.facebook.com/louise.blank.author

Subscribe to my blog: http://louiseblankblog.com

Other books by Louise

MARIGOLDS & MUNCHIES

www.ingramcontent.com/pod-product-compliance
Lightning Source LLC
Chambersburg PA
CBHW060518280326
41933CB00014B/3020